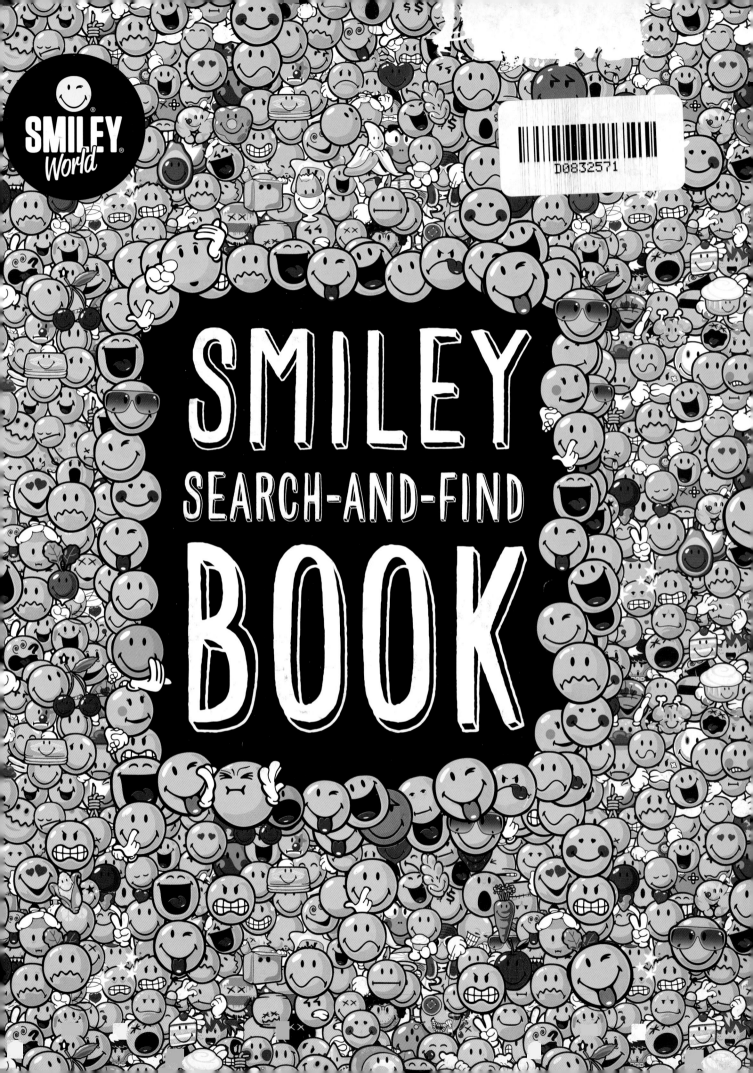

SMILEY
World

SMILEY
SEARCH-AND-FIND
BOOK

Scholastic Children's Books
Euston House, 24 Eversholt Street,
London NW1 1DB, UK

A division of Scholastic Ltd
London ~ New York ~ Toronto ~ Sydney ~ Auckland
Mexico City ~ New Delhi ~ Hong Kong

First published in France by Les Livres du Dragon d'Or, 2009
This edition published in the UK by Scholastic Ltd, 2017

Illustrations: Tim Alan Jones, Qinlu Ye and Haohao Huang
Graphics: Kyung Ah Park
French edition written by Jemma Morgan
UK edition translated by Helen Stokes
Design by Collaborate

ISBN 978 1407 17805 9

Printed in Malaysia

2 4 6 8 10 9 7 5 3 1

www.scholastic.co.uk

Get ready to go search-crazy!

This book takes you on a journey through SmileyWorld and is full of every emoticon you could possibly imagine!

Every time you turn the page you'll discover a new part of SmileyWorld… and in every part of the emoti-packed world there are eight Smileys for you to find:

| love | happiness | confidence | thoughtfulness | anger | embarrassment | sadness | fear |

But be careful! Sometimes the Smileys have taken on a different appearance, just to make your job of catching them more difficult. If you keep a close eye on their expressions, then you should be able to spot them. For example, happiness could look like this:

When you're done, you can check the answers at the back of the book.

SmileyWorld

www.smileyworld.com

STADIUM OF SMILES

In the Smiley Stadium, the grand prix is almost over.

Can you find these eight Smileys before the crowd starts moving and you miss your chance? Tick the boxes as you spot them.

A SPOT OF SHOPPING

Fight your way through the market stalls to find the hiding Smileys. Quickly, before a shopper snaps them up!

PARTY OF THE YEAR!

What an amazing party! Have a great time, but don't lose sight of your mission – can you spot these eight Smileys?

JUNGLE TREK

Make your way to the heart of SmileyWorld jungle. The Smileys you're looking for are well hidden… Beware of wild beasts while you're searching – they may seem gentle but anything can happen in SmileyWorld!

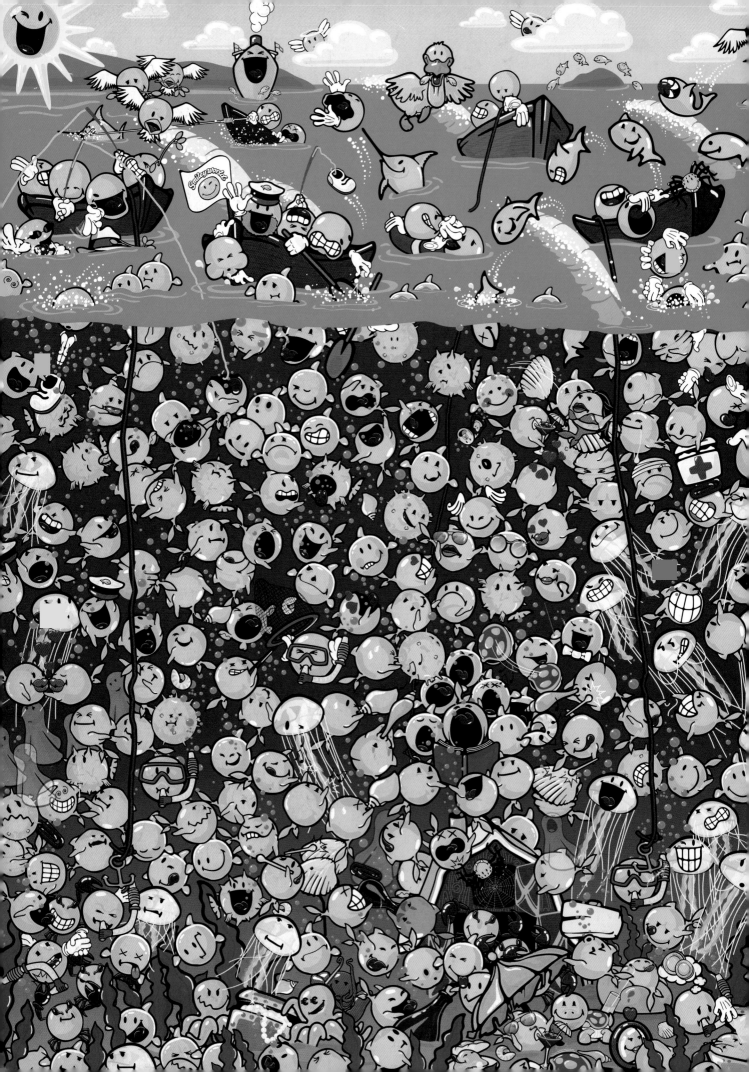

UNDERWATER ADVENTURE

The SmileyWorld sea is a perilous place, teeming with mysterious creatures and hidden treasures. Dive quickly into the deep to find the eight Smileys! Tick them off as you find them.

TIME TO CHAT!

Smileys love chatting online about anything and everything! Feel free to join each conversation – but don't forget to keep an eye out for these eight Smileys:

HALLOWEEN

I.T. GEEKS

GAMES ROOM

JUNK FOOD

BUILDING

FANCY DRESS

SCHOOL

GARDENING

GYMNASTICS

TRAVEL TIPS

WHAT A STORM!

A storm has struck and soaked SmileyWorld. Try to find the hidden eight Smileys before the sun dries them out and they're even harder to spot.

ANNUAL SMILEY GAMES

Smileys from all over the world have come together for the Annual Smiley Games. But something has gone wrong and all the sports are taking place at the same time! Can you find the eight Smileys in amongst the chaos?

BONUS MISSIONS!

Now that you've found all eight Smileys in every part of SmileyWorld, can you find the extra icons on each spread? Tick them off as you find them.

Stadium of Smiles

A Spot of Shopping

Party of the Year!

Jungle Trek

CAN YOU FIND

@ x1

x 64

Circle these on each page when you spot them.

Underwater Adventure

Time to Chat!

What a Storm!

Annual Smiley Games

ANSWERS

STADIUM OF SMILES

Pages 6 and 7

A SPOT OF SHOPPING

Pages 8 and 9

PARTY OF THE YEAR!

JUNGLE TREK

UNDERWATER ADVENTURE

TIME TO CHAT!

Pages 16 and 17

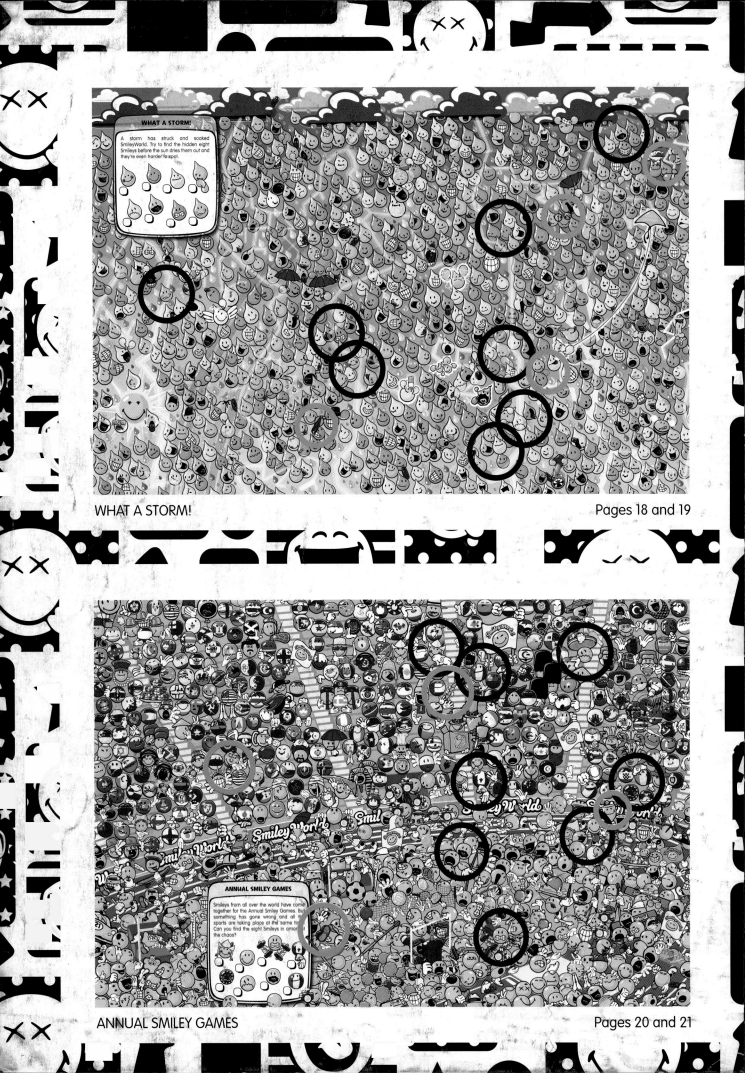

WHAT A STORM!

ANNUAL SMILEY GAMES